THIS NOTEBOOK BELONGS TO

CONTACT

See our range of fine, illustrated books, ebooks, notebooks and art calendars:
www.flametreepublishing.com

This is a **FLAME TREE NOTEBOOK**
Published and © copyright 2018 Flame Tree Publishing Ltd

FTPB 77 • 978-1-78755-063-6

Cover image based on a detail from
Sunburst Gibson Guitar
© Hogan Imaging/Shutterstock.com

Drawing on the specifications of the earlier Les Paul guitars,
Gibson produced this final, antique classic 'Burst' Les Paul before
replacing it with the SG. It features a maple top, mahogany
back and neck, rosewood fingerboard and the acclaimed
1957 Classic PAF humbuckers.

FLAME TREE PUBLISHING l The Art of Fine Gifts
6 Melbray Mews, London SW6 3NS, United Kingdom